New

Praise for *The Power of Crying Out*

"*The Power of Crying Out* will bless and inspire you with a deeper understanding of God's grace and power. Bill Gothard's book has reawakened in me a strong desire to cry out to my Lord with passion and expectancy."

—DR. GARY SMALLEY—

COUNSELOR AND BESTSELLING AUTHOR

"The principles found in *The Power of Crying Out* have made an indelible impact on my life. I have seen them work in the lives of others and would encourage everyone to learn these principles and practice them."

—DR. CHARLES STANLEY—

PASTOR, FIRST BAPTIST CHURCH OF ATLANTA

"Bill Gothard's teaching has been transformational in my life, giving me a foundational understanding of biblical truths, especially on authority. *The Power of Crying Out* explains how God uses crises to bring or keep all of us under the protective authority of God."

—ADRIAN ROGERS—

SENIOR PASTOR, BELLEVUE BAPTIST CHURCH, MEMPHIS, TENNESSEE

"How easy it is to mistake our reluctance to be humble before God for His reluctance to answer our prayers! In *The Power of Crying Out,* Bill Gothard will show you how much God wants to hear from you, and how powerfully He will act when you call to Him with all your heart. This book can change your life."

—BRUCE WILKINSON—

AUTHOR OF THE *NEW YORK TIMES* #1 BESTSELLER

THE PRAYER OF JABEZ

"I can't believe I've overlooked this mighty prayer weapon. *The Power of Crying Out* has convinced me to change and to expect revolutionary results."

—JOHN D. BECKETT—

CHAIRMAN & CEO, R. W. BECKETT CORP.

"*The Power of Crying Out* is a prescription for explosive and effective prayer. James tells us that the 'effectual, fervent prayer of a righteous man availeth much,' and as Bill has explained to me, you can't shout complacently! I'm convinced the Lord is pleased with our loud, fervent, and consistent prayer. My deep thanks to Bill Gothard."

—PAT BOONE—

ENTERTAINER AND AUTHOR

"Bill Gothard, whom I have loved, admired, and respected for many years, has been crying out to God for my physical healing, for which I am deeply grateful. In *The Power of Crying Out,* he describes the scriptural principle of fervent, audible prayer to God—and how many times this is what He is waiting for to bless us mightily and deepen our faith."

—DR. BILL BRIGHT—

FOUNDER, CAMPUS CRUSADE FOR CHRIST

"Until God's people cry out in desperation, there will be little hope for revival. The truth recaptured in this book could be used of God to recapture our nation."

—BYRON PAULUS—

PRESIDENT, LIFE ACTION MINISTRIES

"During the Vietnam War, I was a prisoner of war for seven years; nearly half that in solitary confinement. Captive in leg irons for eighteen months, all I could do was cry out to the Lord. I would not have survived were it not for God's grace, peace, and goodness. Bill Gothard has since helped me grow even closer to God. His excellent teaching has significantly impacted my faith. I know that *The Power of Crying Out* will do the same for those who are blessed to read it."

—SAM JOHNSON—

U.S. CONGRESSMAN, TEXAS,
AND COLONEL, RETIRED, U.S. AIR FORCE

"Bill Gothard is synonymous with a rapier-like penetration of every aspect of the dedicated Christian life. In *The Power of Crying Out,* he provides a refreshing new discernment of the power of effectual praying. Gothard's anecdotal approach to the kind of prayer that gets real answers from God makes for lively and rewarding reading."

—D. JAMES KENNEDY—

SENIOR MINISTER,
CORAL RIDGE PRESBYTERIAN CHURCH

"Bill Gothard's *The Power of Crying Out* will touch the lives of those who read it. The message reminds us that our true source of strength and wisdom lies in humbling ourselves as we cry out to the Lord."

—JIM RYUN—

U.S. CONGRESSMAN, KANSAS

THE POWER *of* CRYING OUT

LIFECHANGE BOOKS

BILL GOTHARD

Multnomah® Publishers *Sisters, Oregon*

THE POWER OF CRYING OUT
published by Multnomah Publishers, Inc.

International Standard Book Number: 1-59052-037-8

Cover image by Age Fotostock

Italics in Scripture quotations are the author's emphasis.

Printed in the United States of America

For information:
MULTNOMAH PUBLISHERS, INC.•POST OFFICE BOX 1720•SISTERS, OREGON 97759

Library of Congress Cataloging-in-Publication Data

Gothard, Bill.
The power of crying out / Bill Gothard.
p. cm.
ISBN 1-59052-037-8
1. Invocation. 2. Prayer--Christianity. I. Title.
BV210.3 .G67 2002
248.3'2--dc21 2002005551

02 03 04 05 06 07 08—10 9 8 7 6 5 4 3

Table of Contents

To all those who are of the household of faith
and to the goal of knowing more of the love
and power of God as we experience
His responses to our cries and fervent prayers.

—**Bill Gothard**

Acknowledgments

I am greatly indebted to my godly father and mother who are now with the Lord. Their daily prayers kept me aware of the reality and power of God.

I am also grateful to a praying Board of Directors and thousands of staff and friends who have invested so much into my life. I especially appreciate Dr. Bruce Wilkinson whose faith and counsel initiated this book, the special encouragement of Don Jacobson, and the insightful and skillful work of Larry Libby and Thomas Womack who made this book a reality.

Introduction

In the Day of Trouble

In the day of my trouble I will call upon You,
for You will answer me.

Psalm 86:7

THE WORLD WILL LONG REMEMBER SEPTEMBER 11, 2001.

Most people will remember that date for the horrific terrorist attacks against the Pentagon and the World Trade Center towers that claimed thousands of innocent lives. Twenty-year-old Anna will remember the day for another reason as well. On that very day, she walked into a medical clinic and began treatment for a deadly cancer that had invaded her body.

The oldest daughter of ten children—in a single parent family—Anna began experiencing excruciating pain in her hip early in August. On September 11, while the world reeled over the news of the attacks on America, Anna began chemotherapy for Hodgkin's lymphoma—which had spread to her bones.

Yes, the doctor had recommended a treatment plan...

but prospects were not at all hopeful. Anna struggled with side effects from several pain medications—including morphine. Her weight had plunged, and she experienced so much pain that she needed assistance just to walk across the room. Her cancer was so far advanced that there was little likelihood of turning it back.

Anna had worked on the headquarter's staff for the Institute in Basic Life Principles. She had also spent time in Romania, serving students and orphans in that impoverished nation.

Stunned and grieved by the shocking turn of events in her young life, Anna called for her church elders to anoint her and pray for her. Here at the ministry, we too were devastated. Gathering as a staff, we cried aloud to the Lord: "O Lord, Abba Father, deliver Anna from cancer and raise her up for Your glory, in the name of Jesus!"

On Christmas Day, Anna recalled the account of the widow pleading her case before the unjust judge,[1] and spent the day crying out to God.

Two days later, she and her mother returned to the doctor. After reviewing the tests used to monitor the cancer, the astounded oncologist declared that she was cancer free! According to the tests, there was no trace left of an aggressive cancer that had already reached stage 4B, the final stage before death. Soon after that appointment, Anna returned to the ski slopes!

What had we done? We had cried out to God. We lifted our voices together, seeking His mercy, His power, and His healing. And He heard and answered with a true medical miracle. (Just ask her doctor.)

Did it matter that we *cried out* to God, calling on Him with *loud voices?*

That is what this little book is all about.

One

Loud and Clear

Lift up your voice with strength,
lift it up, be not afraid.

Isaiah 40:9

AFTER KNOWING THE LORD JESUS CHRIST and teaching and studying His Word for many years, it was only recently that I made what was for me a life-changing discovery.

I saw that the Bible makes a distinction between "prayer" and "crying out to God."

What I have noticed since that time is that He will arrange or allow circumstances to arise that seem to have no solution—and then do nothing to remove the problem.

Until I cry out.

And not one second sooner!

Each situation seems so hopeless, and sometimes a cry seems so futile. Yet this is precisely the setting God wants in order to demonstrate His loving care and His powerful hand of protection.

Sometimes a cry will bring freedom from emotional

bondage; in other cases, God will provide healing from a dread disease, help in a moment of grave danger, or clear direction in a season of deep perplexity.

In every circumstance, the need to cry out is a humbling reminder of my total inability to accomplish anything significant for God. And the result of crying out is a wonderful demonstration of His supernatural power to achieve all that is needed.

His promise to the prophet so long ago is just as true for us in these uncertain days of the twenty-first century:

> "Call to Me, and I will answer you, and show you great and mighty things, which you do not know." (Jeremiah 33:3)

Incredible as it seems, the Creator of the universe desires an intimate, loving fellowship with the people He created. A vital component of that fellowship, as we will discover in these pages, is the actual voicing aloud to Him of our need for Him—particularly in times of great trouble.

In moments of fear, anxiety, and trouble, the right step toward experiencing God's powerful deliverance and protection is to simply cry out—to use our voice in fervent appeal for His help.

All of this may be something of a surprise to you. You may be thinking, *But why is that necessary? Doesn't Scripture tell us that God knows our hearts? When we utter a prayer in our heart or mind, surely there's no critical need to express aloud what God already knows.*

That's all true, of course. He does know our hearts. And He can hear the faintest whisper for help rising from the deepest places of our spirit.

And yet it's strange....

As we survey the Bible with our eyes and hearts wide open, we can't help seeing an unmistakable principle and pattern. God's people, in their time of need, cry out *with their voices* for His help, and He promptly answers with His saving power.

This doesn't happen once or twice, but over and over again.

But it isn't just people in the pages of Scripture who experience this phenomenon. It's still happening to this very day.

A BOLDNESS TAKES OVER

The Dallas Morning News recently carried the following article by columnist Steve Blow, under the headline, "Gunman Faces off with Prayer's Power":

> Sherman Jackson was a little late for the share service at his church on a recent Sunday night.
>
> But that was OK. He had quite a story to share once he got there.
>
> Sherman, 36, and his 7-year-old daughter, Alexa, had stopped for gas on their way to church....

As they were about to drive away, a 30-ish fellow walked up. "Hey, man, I need your help," he said. "Could you please help me jump-start my car? I'll pay you to help me."

Sherman fretted a moment about being late for church. Then he chided himself for thinking of that over helping someone.

So he invited the fellow to get in the front seat. Alexa was in back. And they drove off.

They hadn't gone far when the man reached into his pocket. "I thought he was trying to get out some change to pay me for helping him," Sherman said. But no.

"He pulled out a revolver with his right hand and placed his left hand on my shoulder. He pointed the revolver into my rib cage and said, "OK, man, this is for real. You give me all of your money right now, or I'm going to unload this gun on you."

Sherman was terrified, of course. And mad at himself for putting his daughter in danger.

"OK, look, here's all I have on me," he said, pulling out his money clip.

"Take it all."

But the robber didn't believe him. "That's not all. Give it all to me," he said, shoving the gun harder into Sherman's ribs.

Sherman, a Garland insurance agent, keeps

Gideon Bibles in his car with a dollar bill tucked in each one. He gives them to the homeless. The gunman spotted one of those bills sticking out and began to scream at Sherman:

"You lied to me! There is more money here."

Something came over Sherman just then, and he began to pray out loud. "Father in heaven, hear my cry and deliver me from this present evil. . . ."

He felt a sudden calm. "I lost all consciousness of concern and worry," he said. "A boldness took over."

He slowed the car and began to make a U-turn. The gunman screamed, "What are you doing?"

"This car is being turned around," Sherman replied, "and I am not taking orders from you anymore."

The man put the gun against Sherman's chest. "You don't get it, man. You mean nothing to me. I'll pull this trigger."

"No, you don't understand," Sherman cut him off. "Greater is He that is in me than he that is in the world. My Jesus is stronger than your gun."

He could see the gunman tug on the trigger. The hammer drew back. But Sherman didn't flinch. He pulled over and stopped.

"I want to tell you about Jesus," he said to the gunman.

The man wavered a moment, lowered his gun, and then dropped his head. When he looked up, he was crying. "I'm so sorry, man. I'm so, so sorry," he said. "I was going to shoot you."

"Don't worry about it. I forgive you," Sherman said. And then he began to tell the man about new life through belief in Jesus.

Sherman urged the man to go on to church with him, but he declined. He asked Sherman to drive him to his car at a store.

Along the way, the man began to tell Sherman about all his problems. He said his name was Mike and reached out to shake Sherman's hand. Sherman continued talking to him about starting life anew with God.

As they neared the grocery, Sherman said, "And by the way, Mike, I want my money clip back."

"Do what?!" Mike exclaimed. But then he meekly handed it over.

"And," Sherman went on, "you are keeping this New Testament, and you are going to read it like you never read anything else before. And I'm going to be praying for you, Mike, that God will come into your life."

They pulled alongside Mike's car. "He got out," Sherman said, "with the revolver in one hand, the Bible in the other hand, and tears in his eyes."

And Sherman drove on to church.[2]

Some readers wrote to the columnist to say they didn't believe this story. A follow-up article in the same newspaper, however, revealed that "Mike" was suspected of involvement in "a rash of 15 or so nearly identical robberies in the area." Police officers informed Sherman that he was the only one who got his money back. A few weeks later, Mike was captured and is now in regular contact with Sherman.

In that frightening moment when a gun was thrust into his chest and Sherman Jackson uttered his cry to God, he was following a pattern repeated throughout God's Word—and throughout history. God heard and acted—just as He has responded again and again to His people's cries.

And just as He longs to respond to you.

Points to Ponder

Does your prayer life have the power that you want it to have? Do you ever wonder why some of your prayers don't seem to reach "the ears of God"? Do you want to experience greater results from your prayers?

Two

GOD HEARS!

I love the LORD,
because He has heard my voice.

PSALM 116:1

FOR MOST OF MY LIFE, I assumed that crying out was simply synonymous with prayer. I've come to be amazed, however, to see the specific purposes and potential for crying out—and how this is emphasized time and again in Scripture.

God hears our prayers, and the Bible's testimony reveals that, in a special way, He particularly hears us when our requests are voiced *aloud.*

Many believers today seem unaware of this consistent pattern in God's Word. It could even be said that the most significant difference between the prayers of God's saints in Scripture (so powerfully effective) and our prayers today (so seemingly ineffective) is this: *The prayers of biblical saints were much more often spoken out loud—with corresponding fervency.*

When we grasp this fact, the pages of Scripture come

alive with sound! We encounter men and women in the Bible truly trusting that *God hears,* and giving voice to their requests and praises. Earnestly believing this, these believers of old filled His ears with the cries from their hearts that flowed out through their lips.

FROM WHISPERS TO SHOUTS

Both the Old and New Testaments employ an amazing variety of words to describe human communication with God. In most cases the inherent meaning in these words includes some sort of audible sound—an aspect that doesn't always come across as strongly in the English translations.

The kind of sounds implied by these words varies—anything from a low whisper or moan all the way to ear-splitting shouts. In approaching God, these saints of old brought a wide range of emotions and mind-sets that were reflected in the tone and pitch and volume of their freely-spoken prayers.

Words for prayer that have a built-in meaning of audible sound are particularly evident in passages that promise God's hearing. The verse I cited earlier is an example: "*Call* to Me," the Lord invites His people through the prophet Jeremiah, "and I will answer you, and show you great and mighty things, which you do not know."

The first word here is the Hebrew *qara,* which generally carries the meaning of calling aloud or crying out. The same word begins an invitation and promise found in the Psalms— "*Call* upon Me in the day of trouble; I will deliver you, and you shall glorify Me."[3] David used this *qara* word often, as in these lines: "The LORD is near to all who *call* upon Him, to all who *call* upon Him in truth."[4]

AN OUTFLOW, NOT A FORMULA

No one in Scripture shows more vital faith in the God who hears than David, the man after God's own heart. In one psalm he states, "Evening and morning and at noon I will pray, and *cry aloud,* and *He shall hear my voice.*"[5] The Hebrew word here for crying aloud is *hamah,* with the connotation of a loud humming or murmuring—even to a growl or roar.

"In my distress," David says elsewhere, *"I called* upon the LORD, and *cried out* to my God; *He heard my voice* from His temple, and *my cry* came before Him, even to His ears."[6] Here the word for David's outcry is *shava,* connoting a higher-pitched shout for help. David assures us, "The eyes of the LORD are on the righteous, and His ears are open to their *cry.*"[7]

An actual shriek, as if in grief, is the root meaning of the word *tsa'aq,* which David uses in these lines: "The righteous *cry out,* and the LORD hears, and delivers them out of all their troubles."[8] And a ringing or shrill sound is conveyed in the word *rinnah,* which David chose to loudly plead, "Hear my *cry,* O God."[9]

Repeatedly, David found in his experience that what he uttered aloud with such deep and sincere emotion, God heard: *"I cried* to the LORD *with my voice,* and *He heard me* from His holy hill.... O LORD my God, *I cried out to You,* and *You healed me.*"[10]

Over and over David demonstrates his trust that God would hear him yet again: *"The LORD will hear* when *I call* to Him.... *To You I will cry,* O LORD my Rock.... Hear the voice of my supplications *when I cry to You.*"[11]

Can there be any doubt? David clearly means us to understand that his prayers are actually sounded out: "I *cry out* to the LORD *with my voice; with my voice* to the LORD I make my supplication."[12]

The son of Jesse spoke his prayers aloud with faith and fervency. Praying aloud was no mechanical formula or gimmick or "lucky rabbit's foot" with David.

It was a natural outflow of a love relationship with his listening Lord.

CHILD TO FATHER

This can be true for you and me as well. Today. Right now.

The more we believe in the ongoing miracle that *God actually hears us*—through the way opened up for us into His sanctuary by Christ's blood—the more freely and fervently we'll give voice to our prayers...to the delight of our Father's heart.

We know from our own families that a true father's heart hears his children's cries, and that the children naturally cry to him. In the same way, crying out to God is our child-to-Father impulse, planted in our hearts by the Holy Spirit within us.

"Because you are sons," Paul teaches us in the New Testament, "God has sent forth the Spirit of His Son into your hearts, *crying out,* 'Abba, Father!'"[13] The Greek verb used here for crying out is a strong word, usually translated as "shouting." The Holy Spirit Himself is at work within us to prompt our crying out aloud to God. And because God is compassionate, gracious, and always faithful to His promise, He will indeed hear and answer these cries that He Himself inspires.

Points to Ponder

Have you ever found yourself deliberately suppressing the urge to cry out to your heavenly Father? Could it be that you've quenched the Spirit of God by this action? If so, it's time to make a change—and respond to Him in humility and obedience.

Three

THE GIFT OF VOICE

"Let me hear your voice."

SONG OF SOLOMON 2:14

HE WHO WANTS YOUR HEART also wants your voice.

Praying aloud is a natural way to give *more* to God, to love Him *more*...to pray to Him not just with your heart and mind, but also with your vocal energy. Like fasting or kneeling, crying out is a Scripture-sanctioned way to pray with intensity and commitment.

SURROUNDED WITH SOUND

The saints of old wanted to make sure they used their voices for what mattered most. Not only prayer, but even reading was commonly done aloud in ancient times. We see an example of that in Acts 8, with the chariot-riding Ethiopian, whom Philip heard reading aloud from the prophet Isaiah while traveling on the desert road.

Did you know that even meditation was a vocal exercise? We think of meditating as sitting silently under a tree, or by a crackling fire, with an open Bible before us. In the Old Testament, however, the Hebrew words for "meditate" and "meditation" (from the root *hagah*) actually refer to a low murmur. In fact, the word is used in Scripture for the low rumbling growl of a lion after catching its prey,[14] for the moan of a dove,[15] and for the sound of human mourning.[16]

Sometimes in the Psalms and Proverbs, this word *hagah* is actually translated as "speak"—"And my tongue shall *speak* of Your righteousness"; "The mouth of the righteous *speaks* wisdom"; "For my mouth will *speak* truth."[17] It wasn't the term for normal speaking, but implied a lower, repetitive sound.

It seems likely, then, that during the biblical process of meditation, memorized Scriptures were actually spoken aloud to help the heart and mind engage with God's truth. So when the Lord told Joshua, "This Book of the Law shall not depart *from your mouth,* but you shall *meditate* [*hagah*] in it day and night,"[18] the actual sounding out of the Scriptures from his mouth (with focused mental attention) was what Joshua knew to do.

The same is true for the person to whom blessing is promised in the first psalm—the one whose "delight is in the law of the LORD, and in His law he *meditates* day and night."[19] This person would continually and delightedly sound forth in a low but intense voice the Scripture he loved.

Surely this greater blessing can also be ours as we meditate with the same demonstrated intensity—just like the heightened blessing that can accompany spoken prayer.

IN A NOISY WORLD

Ours is a loud and noisy world, and the volume keeps getting cranked up higher.

Our blaring, honking, screaming, shouting, babbling, ranting world competes with genuine words of prayer uttered to our loving God. *But once these beautiful sounds are made, they cannot be prevented from reaching His ears.* They can never be drowned out or overpowered by the world's harsh and ceaseless noise.

What a privilege we have! We possess the authority and permission and right—as God's adopted sons and daughters—to boldly speak before our Father in heaven, in unbroken access to His throne. And the Holy Spirit works within us to accomplish exactly that: "For you did not receive the spirit of bondage again to fear, but you received the Spirit of adoption by whom *we cry out,* 'Abba, Father.'"[20]

By crying out, we let our own voices join in harmony with the voice of Christ, "who is…at the right hand of God, who also makes intercession for us."[21]

It can be humbling to use our voices this much in prayer.

As we call aloud our prayers, we can more easily recognize our heart's condition before God. Hearing our own spoken words, we quickly detect any lack of fervency or humility or reverence. Listening to ourselves, we're forced to examine our hearts. And this is good.

THE UNVOICED CRY

Obviously, God isn't hard-of-hearing. He can hear the faintest silent cry of the heart. Even if it's only a passing thought. Even if it's only a groan without words.[22] Can you hear a longing? God does. And His ears don't miss a single sigh that escapes our lips.[23] Though we're focusing on the cry actually uttered to God, you can see examples of voiceless prayers in the Scriptures too.

Who can forget, for example, the desperate woman who crept near to Jesus in the pressing, jostling crowd. The whole extent of her "prayer" was to simply and silently touch the border of His robe. As she did so, believing she would be healed of her chronic hemorrhaging, she received the very desire of her heart.[24]

Sometimes a person prays with his tears, even when words are missing. Hannah came with a burdened heart to the Lord's tabernacle. "And she was in bitterness of soul, and prayed to the LORD and wept in anguish." Eli, the Lord's priest, saw her praying there.

"And it happened, as she continued praying before the LORD, that Eli watched her mouth. Now Hannah spoke in her heart; only her lips moved, but her voice was not heard." When Eli questioned her, she answered, "I...have poured out my soul before the LORD."[25]

Though Hannah's physical voice was silent, God heard her fervent, poured-out prayer in that place and granted her a son. Little Samuel grew up to become one of the Lord's most dedicated servants—and a mighty prayer warrior himself.

Charles Spurgeon once preached a sermon called "Wordless Prayers Heard in Heaven," and used Isaiah 41:17 as his text—where the poor and needy are so thirsty that their voices are gone, but God in His mercy says, *"I, the LORD, will hear them;* I, the God of Israel, will not forsake them."[26]

But more frequent in Scripture is the example and encouragement of truly crying out to God, using the voice, in sincerity and trust.

Points to Ponder

On a three-by-five card or sticky note, write out several verses from one of the heartfelt prayers in the Psalms. (Some good places to start might include Psalms 16, 23, 25, 31, 51, or 63.) Make each verse your own prayer—out loud—several times a day over the course of the week. See if this increases your concentration and fervency in prayer.

Four

The Climax to All the Best Stories

"Your fathers cried out to the Lord."

1 Samuel 12:8

SOME MONTHS AGO, a nineteen-year-old Russian boy named Dima dived into a shallow river. He broke his neck and back, punctured a lung, and sustained other internal injuries. He was taken to the nearest hospital, many miles away, where doctors concluded there was no way he could survive.

Dima had visited our ministry headquarters several years earlier, so when we learned about this incident, we realized it would be a wonderful opportunity for God to show His power. Therefore we cried out, "O God, deliver Dima from death and raise him up for Your glory." We also contacted others in our ministry network and urged them to cry out for Dima, which they did.

A week later, we talked with Dima's grandmother, who

thanked us for crying out, and announced that the doctors had now reversed their prognosis. Dima would live. He is receiving therapy and learning to use his hands and arms.

When we call out to the Lord for His mighty help in the face of an impossible situation, we are following in the footsteps of both Old Testament saints and New Testament believers from the very dawn of the church.

Christians in those early days were known as people who *called upon* the name of the Lord. They thought of themselves in those terms,[27] and Paul used that designation for believers as well.[28] This was no randomly chosen description, but a phrase that captured the most exciting dynamics in the long story of God's dealings with His people.

We've begun discovering that the concept of crying out to God is a frequent pattern in Scripture. How often that moment of crying out to God becomes the very turning point and climax of biblical stories dealing with God's deliverance of His people!

THE BIGGEST EPIC

The most honored and remembered Old Testament story of God's salvation was His rescue of His people from slavery in Egypt. What triggered this rescue? Very early in Exodus we read,

> The children of Israel groaned because of the bondage, and *they cried out;* and *their cry came up to God* because of the bondage. So *God heard* their

> groaning, and God remembered His covenant with Abraham, with Isaac, and with Jacob. And God looked upon the children of Israel, and God acknowledged them.[29]

The people cried out to God, and He heard and remembered. In a sense, the story is now already over practically before it begins! The people's rescue from slavery is now assured and guaranteed—a done deal. Already the victory is won. It's only a matter of time until the world sees exactly how the victory plays out.

Right away God clued Moses in on what was happening and why. He said to Moses,

> "I have surely seen the oppression of My people who are in Egypt, and *have heard their cry* because of their taskmasters, for I know their sorrows. So I have come down to deliver them out of the hand of the Egyptians, and to bring them up from that land to a good and large land, to a land flowing with milk and honey."[30]

Moses was given a position of leadership on the side of the guaranteed winner in the coming conflict, though there were still plenty of seemingly impossible hurdles on the horizon. In fact, when their flight from Egypt was halted at the Red Sea, and the people in fear looked back to see approaching chariots from Pharaoh's army, all seemed lost.

But again, "the children of Israel cried out to the LORD,"[31] and God mercifully heard them. And you know what happened next!

MISERY THAT GOD CAN'T ENDURE

In the days of the book of Judges, the people repeatedly disobeyed God and as a result found themselves oppressed by a host of enemies. But the experience of God's deliverance was repeated each time as well. Again and again, a cry from the people triggered it.

> The children of Israel served Cushan-Rishathaim eight years. When the children of Israel *cried out* to the LORD, the LORD raised up a deliverer for the children of Israel, who delivered them: Othniel....
>
> The children of Israel served Eglon king of Moab eighteen years. But when the children of Israel *cried out* to the LORD, the LORD raised up a deliverer for them: Ehud....
>
> And the children of Israel *cried out* to the LORD; for Jabin had nine hundred chariots of iron, and for twenty years he had harshly oppressed the children of Israel. [This time, Deborah was God's chosen deliverer.][32]

Years later, the cycle of their disobedience occurred again, and in this instance the people included repentance in their cry to the Lord:

> The people of Ammon crossed over the Jordan to fight…so that Israel was severely distressed. And the children of Israel *cried out* to the LORD, saying, "We have sinned against You, because we have both forsaken our God and served the Baals!"

This time God's answer was a rebuke:

> "Did I not deliver you from the Egyptians and from the Amorites and from the people of Ammon and from the Philistines? Also the Sidonians and Amalekites and Maonites oppressed you; and you cried out to Me, and I delivered you from their hand. Yet you have forsaken Me and served other gods. Therefore *I will deliver you no more.* Go and cry out to the gods which you have chosen; let them deliver you in your time of distress."

"I will deliver you no more"! So the cycle of the Lord's deliverance of His people at last was broken.

Or was it?

At once the people cried out again:

> "We have sinned! Do to us whatever seems best to You; only deliver us this day, we pray." So they put away the foreign gods from among them and served the LORD.[33]

Would this further cry and accompanying obedience make any difference to God?

Yes. "His soul could no longer endure the misery of Israel."[34] He sent His people yet another deliverer, Jephthah the Gileadite, "a mighty man of valor."[35]

What a picture of the abounding mercy of God; always faithful to His covenant, and ever ready to hear the cry of His covenant people!

THE CRY OF TRUST

In David's day this crying out was the story's main theme as he sang about his nation's past:

> Our fathers trusted in You;
> They trusted, and You delivered them.
> *They cried to You,* and were delivered;
> They trusted in You, and were not ashamed.[36]

But finally Israel's repeated pattern of disobedience caused God to destroy Jerusalem and send His people into captivity in faraway Babylon. There in Babylon, the captive Daniel read from the Scriptures the prophecy given to Jeremiah that this captivity would be over in seventy years. Daniel therefore set his face "toward the Lord God to make request by prayer and supplications, with fasting, sackcloth, and ashes."[37] He cried out to God in humility, worship, and confession and ended his prayer by pleading aloud:

> Now therefore, our God, *hear* the prayer of Your servant, and his supplications.... O my God, *incline Your ear* and *hear;* open Your eyes and see our desolations, and the city which is called by Your name.... O Lord, *hear!* O Lord, forgive! O Lord, *listen* and act! Do not delay for Your own sake, my God, for Your city and Your people are called by Your name.[38]

God indeed listened to the cries of righteous Daniel; soon, in the days of Ezra and Nehemiah, He sent the captives back to Jerusalem to rebuild the city and its walls and the temple.

It is the heartfelt cry that always reconnects the people back to God and His grace and His mercy.

ALL OUR STORIES

Finally, let's look at one more stream of Scripture where crying out to God is the repeated theme—and where God shows us how significant it is to Him.

In Psalm 107, He gives us four descriptions of people in great need, and these serve as pictures of every kind of vulnerability and hardship we might encounter—physically, emotionally, and spiritually.

First we read of those who "wandered in the wilderness in a desolate way," fainting from hunger and thirst.

Then come those "who sat in darkness and in the shadow of death," subjected to prison and bitter labor because of their rebellion against God.

We then read of those who are labeled "fools" because of their sin, and who experienced wasting disease that drew them "near to the gates of death."

Finally, there are the adventurers "who go down to the sea in ships," and who encounter the worst of storms on the ocean, melting their souls in fear.

In all these different scenarios, what would cause God in mercy to reach down with His rescue and release? The psalmist shows us. In all four stories, the turning point and climax is the same:

> Then they cried out to the LORD in their trouble,
> And He delivered them out of their distresses.[39]

Again and again, in story after story—in the Bible's pages and in all history since then—we see God's active involvement triggered by the cry of His people.

Points to Ponder

Read through verse 32 of Psalm 107, thinking about the circumstances of those who "cried out" to the Lord in their great distress. Have you ever found yourself in a similar circumstance? Are you experiencing one now? Cry aloud to God in your trouble—and then "give thanks to the LORD for His goodness" (Psalm 107:8).

Five

In the Hour of Need

"Call upon Me in the day of trouble."

Psalm 50:15

DAYS OF TROUBLE. Hours of crisis. Moments of urgent and fearful need. They come to us all unexpectedly, like a thief in the night. How can we prepare for such times?

We can prepare by being ready to cry aloud to the Lord for His saving help, boldly expecting His deliverance. God invites and expects His beloved ones to do exactly that: *"Call upon Me in the day of trouble,"* He tells us; "I will deliver you, and you shall glorify Me."[40]

Many of us find it humiliating and difficult to cry out for help in times of trouble. Especially men! We prefer to be known as rugged, self-sufficient types. We don't want to ask for directions until we're hopelessly lost. We'd rather endure tenaciously in the face of insurmountable odds and then conclude with pride, *I did it!*

But God's ways are often opposite to our lines of reasoning. He wants us to come to the conclusion, *God did it!*

He asks that we recognize our weakness in order to experience His strength, so we can say with Paul, "When I am weak, then I am strong."[41] And there's no better way to express our weakness than to honestly cry out to God for deliverance in times of trouble.

It takes a lot of humility to cry aloud to God in our distress.

And humility before the living God is precisely what we need.

GETTING OUR ATTENTION

To all His children who cry aloud for help in desperate moments, God still demonstrates again and again that He "is our refuge and strength, *a very present help in trouble.*"[42]

When a farmer in Michigan became prosperous, he rewarded himself with the most efficient, high-powered tractor he could buy. He was using it one day with a conveyor belt to lift crops into a barn loft. Suddenly his sleeve caught in the mechanism, and he was jerked into the path of the large wheel. He realized that in only seconds he would be crushed to death, as had happened to a neighbor in a similar accident only a few weeks before.

He cried out in a loud voice, "O God, save me!"

At that instant the engine stalled. A farmhand came running out and helped free the man from the belt mechanism. They checked the engine, but could find no plausible, mechanical reason for the stall. Together they realized that God had stopped the engine in response to the farmer's cry.

As the farmer publicly gave this report, he also acknowledged that before this experience he hadn't felt his need for the Lord because things were going so well for him. Now he realized that every day was a gift from the Lord; he knew he was "a dead man on furlough."

THE DIFFERENCE IT CAN MAKE

In so many ways, God continues to teach us to be faithful in crying out for His help in our difficulties.

On a wintry day, a father was driving on a southern Illinois highway to visit his son at his university. Suddenly his vehicle began spinning out of control on a patch of ice he hadn't seen, and he was headed for the roadside ditch. He cried out, "O God, deliver me!" Then it was as if a giant hand righted the car back on the road.

The father rejoiced in this deliverance and continued driving. About twenty minutes later, he hit another patch of ice and spun out of control. This time he simply exclaimed, "Oh, no!"—and his vehicle ended up in the ditch. What was God teaching him?

A teenage boy, who stated openly that he didn't believe in God, was asked why. "Our family was going through a very hard time," he explained, "and I prayed that God would help us—but nothing happened."

On the other hand, in another family with a teenager, the father had been out of work for more than a year; though he was actively seeking employment, and his family prayed consistently for a job for him. His teenage daughter discussed the family's problem with me, and I suggested some ideas for employment for her father. She then passed along these ideas to him.

In response, he carefully explained why each suggestion wouldn't work. The girl's hopes for a solution vanished.

Later that day, she walked out to a quiet place, where she did more than pray. She cried out, "O God, deliver my father from unemployment!" The next day her father was offered an excellent job and started to work immediately.

The father in another family had this testimony:

> I was $20,000 in debt with unsecured loans. For two years I had been trying to sell some land to cover the debt, but I couldn't even get a phone call of interest. I tried realtor after realtor without success.
>
> Finally, in desperation, I walked into the woods and cried, "O God!" That's all that came out. My voice failed as emotion flooded me, and I groaned in my spirit.
>
> The next day, a couple told my wife they'd heard we had land for sale. Within twenty-four hours of crying out, we had an agreement to sell the land for $20,000. Praise God! We are now debt-free and living by God's financial principles.

AFFLICTED AND OVERWHELMED

By crying aloud in the day of trouble, we follow in the steps of Christ, our teacher. For Jesus, the "day of trouble" came most heavily that late night in Gethsemane and in the succeeding hours that ended with His death on the cross. Facing a time more troubling than any we could ever imagine, Jesus cried aloud.

By crying out, we also follow the example of many others in Scripture.

Psalm 102 is titled "A Prayer of the afflicted, when he is overwhelmed and pours out his complaint before the LORD." Those words *afflicted* and *overwhelmed* may not carry much weight for you at this moment; they're easy to read over lightly. But the hour comes in each of our lives when words like that leap out at us and catch exactly our heart's condition. In that very moment, we can confidently call out to God, just as the psalmist did:

> Hear my prayer, O LORD,
> And *let my cry come to You.*
> Do not hide Your face from me *in the day of my trouble;*
> Incline Your ear to me;
> In the day that I call, *answer me speedily.*[43]

The disciples of Jesus knew what it was like to feel overwhelmed by trouble. One day on the Sea of Galilee, as wind and water battered their boat, they realized this was no ordinary storm. Their vessel was filling fast with water, and they fully expected to drown. Jesus was in the boat with them, yet somehow remained fast asleep.

Reaching total desperation—feeling afflicted and overwhelmed—they cried out to Him: "Lord, save us! We are perishing!" Only then did Jesus act to still the storm.[44]

So it is many times with us: Only when we cry out to Him in desperation does He calm the storms in our lives.

DESPERATE MOMENTS

It was the same for Peter on another occasion on the Sea of Galilee, as he was actually walking on the water toward Jesus, at his Lord's invitation. "But when he saw that the wind was boisterous, he was afraid; and beginning to sink *he cried out,* saying, 'Lord, save me!'" At the moment of Peter's cry, "immediately Jesus stretched out His hand and caught him."[45]

Jonah's "day of trouble" landed him in the belly of a great fish, and even there he managed to let his voice sound forth. *"I cried out to the LORD* because of my affliction, and He answered me. Out of the belly of Sheol I cried, and *You heard my voice."*[46]

Throughout their generations in the Promised Land, the nation of Israel faced impossible circumstances for survival in desperate conflicts with the well-armed forces of their pagan enemies. But as they lifted their voices to beseech the Lord, He delivered them. "*They cried out to God* in the battle. He heeded their prayer, because they put their trust in Him."[47]

TOO TROUBLED TO PRAY?

Some people speak of times when their personal circumstances are so oppressive and despairing that they cannot even pray silently—let alone cry out to God.

Perhaps their condition can be compared to that of Heman the Ezrahite, who wrote a psalm which is the darkest and most depressed chapter in all the Psalms. He described his situation with phrases like these: "full of troubles…near to the grave…adrift among the dead…in the lowest pit, in darkness, in the depths…shut up, and I cannot get out…afflicted and ready to die…distraught…engulfed."[48]

He was entirely alone and abandoned, and his closing line in this psalm is translated with these words (in various Scripture versions): "My companions have become darkness"; "There is only darkness everywhere"; "My acquaintances are in darkness."[49] May we ourselves never have to experience such total gloom!

Yet even in this dungeon of depression, look what this man in faith was able to do and say:

His psalm begins,

O LORD, God of my salvation,
I have *cried out day and night* before You.
Let my prayer come before You;
Incline Your ear to my cry.

Before God, he could testify this:

> LORD, I have *called daily* upon You;
> I have stretched out my hands to You.

And this:

> But to You I *have cried out,* O LORD,
> And in the morning my prayer comes before You.[50]

From this troubled man's personal journal we're wise to learn that we *never* face a darkness so deep that we cannot cry out to God.

GOD HEARS THOSE IN GREAT NEED

We see in Scripture that the greater someone's helplessness and need, the more God seems to emphasize His commitment to hear their cry in trouble. God affirms His special concern for the fatherless, widows, strangers (foreigners), and the poor—people with exceptional needs and crises that others do not experience.

God testified to Moses that if oppressed widows and orphans called out to Him, "I will surely hear their *cry.*"[51] Solomon said that God "will deliver the needy when he *cries,* the poor also, and him who has no helper."[52]

God's compassion in such cases of special hardship is something He expects us to share as well. He tells us, "Whoever shuts his ears to the cry of the poor will also cry himself and not be heard."[53] And He warned Moses and the people at Sinai, "You shall not afflict any widow or fatherless child. If you afflict them in any way, and *they cry at all to Me, I will surely hear their cry;* and My wrath will become hot, and I will kill you with the sword; your wives shall be widows, and your children fatherless."[54] He likewise warned them not to withhold wages or otherwise oppress a poor hired servant, "lest he *cry out against you* to the LORD, and it be sin to you."[55]

God is utterly serious about hearing those in destitution who cry out to Him in their trouble!

KNOW AND BELIEVE

So, from Scripture you can know this and believe it in every difficulty you face: God delights in showing Himself strong on behalf of anyone who is facing an impossible situation and who will cry out for His deliverance.

As you cry aloud to Him...

May the LORD answer you in the day of trouble;
May the name of the God of Jacob defend you.[56]

Points to Ponder

Think of two areas in your personal life where you have felt totally helpless to make a change. Take those two points of weakness and cry out to the Lord for wisdom, strength, and deliverance!

Six

For Great and Mighty Things

"Call to Me, and I will answer you,
and show you great and mighty things,
which you do not know."

Jeremiah 33:3

IN HIS INFINITE COMPASSION, God answers our cry and meets our needs. In doing so, He often goes far beyond all that we could ever ask or imagine. How great is our God!

FOR POWER IN HOLY AND RIGHTEOUS LIVING

Many men wrestle in particular with two of the enemy's stormy strongholds—the violence of anger and the passion of sexual lust.

On a June morning in a convention center in Knoxville, Tennessee, several thousand men dealt with this situation by getting on their knees and crying out in one loud voice, *"Abba, Father, in the name of Jesus, deliver me from anger and lust!"*

The effectiveness of that cry is reported in the following letter, written a few months later by a man who said anger and lust "had been particularly devastating in my life, affecting my relationships with people that were closest to me."

> That Friday as we all knelt in the auditorium, I was overwhelmed by my absolute helplessness to overcome the least little habit—much less a great giant that had dominated so much of my life. I broke down in tears as the two or three thousand men there at the convention center began crying out to God for deliverance and victory. With all my heart (in great hopelessness of my own abilities) I cried out to Him, "Abba, Father…Daddy!"
>
> Even now as I write this, I am overcome with emotion. I walked away from there and I felt no immediate change. But as I returned home something was different. There was a measurable decrease in the influence of temptation. There was a new freedom and feeling of victory for the first time in my life. Now when I am tempted I can actually think, *I am not afraid!* and I calmly praise the Lord because He hath given me the victory this day! My heart is overwhelmed with joy. I've been freed from that prison.

Another cry for help brought victory for a man who wrote this:

> I have long been held captive by lust. In the third grade, while walking home from school, I picked up what looked like a comic book. It was my first exposure to pornography. My young heart was captured.
>
> Lust nearly ruined my marriage on numerous occasions. I truly wanted to be free from it and confessed it many times to God. I even sought help from Christian counselors.
>
> In May 2001, your message on crying out was given at our men's meeting. For two more weeks I struggled with lust. Finally, on the way to work, I stopped the car and cried out to God for deliverance from lust. God was faithful, and the bondage has been broken.

David says, "In the day when I *cried out,* You answered me, and made me bold with strength in my soul."[57] God wants us to cry out to Him for the strength of soul available through His Spirit to break the bonds of unrighteousness in our lives.

Trying to live the Christian life by our own strength is impossible! A quick look at just a few biblical commands confirms this fact.

- Love your enemies, do good to those who hate you…
- Be perfect…

- Be complete…
- Walk worthy…with all lowliness, gentleness, and longsuffering…
- Be holy…
- Pray without ceasing…
- Love the Lord your God with all your heart, with all your soul, with all your strength, and with all your mind, and your neighbor as yourself.[58]

We have to come face to face with the futility of our own efforts to meet such standards—apart from the Holy Spirit's enablement as we abide in Christ. Such realization spurs us on to cry out for that enablement and that abiding. We cry out for the Lord's help when we realize that what's required of us is vastly beyond our abilities.

FOR WISDOM

Early in the book of Proverbs we're told to *"cry out* for discernment, and *lift up your voice* for understanding."[59]

A few years ago, some men in our ministry were preparing for a father-son camp out. On some heavily forested area of our ministry property, th[illegible] were instructed to cut down some midsized trees to be [illegible] an outdoor amphitheater. Unfortunate[illegible] take a number of trees from a neig[illegible] property line was unmarked, and our [illegible] his on three sides, so their mistake w[illegible]

However, when the neighbor lear[illegible]

he accused us of *intentionally* cutting them—and demanded $7,000 in payment.

We knew the trees were nowhere near this value, so we called in a log assessor who estimated their price at about $860 at most. We then called our neighbor and offered him what we believed was a just amount. He stood firm on his demand, claiming that the young men knowingly trespassed on his property. He gave us a deadline for the payment and threatened to take us to court if we didn't meet it.

On the day of the deadline, I reviewed our situation. The more I looked at the problem, the more impossible it seemed. The $7,000 price was far too unreasonable. On the other hand, we *were* guilty. And going to court would consume valuable time, cost thousands of dollars in legal fees, and result in an even greater rift with our neighbor.

What could we do? There was no good solution for us. I knew I had to phone the neighbor and talk further with him, but what should I say?

God reminded me that this was a time to cry out. I got on my face before the Lord and cried out in a loud voice, "O Lord, Abba, Father, deliver us from this situation!"

As soon as I finished my cry, two words clearly came to my mind.

Buy it.

At first, I didn't understand their significance, so I [illegible]d them in my mind: *Buy it.... Buy it? Oh—buy the*

I then called the neighbor, who immediately started rehearsing his view of the situation. I assured him we would do what was right and then asked him when he had obtained the land.

"In 1952," he replied.

I asked him what his purpose had been in obtaining it.

"We got it for an investment."

"Have you ever thought about selling it?" I inquired.

"For the right price."

"What's the right price?"

"Fifteen thousand dollars."

This was amazing! I tried to remain calm. That was only $8,000 more than he wanted for the trees we took! It was a good-sized tract of beautiful, wooded property with a road in front and a stream in back.

I told him I would check on some things and call him right back.

I hung up the phone, thought things through, and made sure of the ministry's authorization for such a purchase, then quickly called the neighbor back.

"We'll buy your property at your price."

"Fine," he said.

"This will solve our whole problem, won't it?"

"It certainly will!" he replied. The sale was soon finalized.

Later, because of a mistake by the title company in defining an easement, we were given $5,000 in compensation for their error. Thus, for only $3,000 more than the neighbor originally wanted for the trees, we purchased his entire tract of land—forty acres!

I'm confident it would never have been on my mind to buy it had I not cried out to God in what was a hopeless situation.

FOR SELF-CONTROL

Ken Pierpont knew that self-control was a good character quality. As a pastor, he even gave sermons on the subject. However, it was quite obvious to his congregation and to his doctor that he hadn't learned this quality.

One day he attended a birthday party for his mother-in-law. One of the birthday gifts was a floor scale. The party guests took turns stepping on it to weigh themselves. When Ken stood on the scales, it read "Error." He took things out of his pockets and took off his shoes and belt. Finally, it registered a weight—three hundred pounds!

Ken had tried many different weight-loss programs and diets to solve his problem, but nothing worked. He even fasted for forty days and lost about forty pounds, but a few weeks later the weight was back on. He read books on nutrition and tried to change his eating habits, but always slipped back into his old ways.

One morning, Ken looked in the mirror and realized all his efforts were hopeless and there was only one thing left to do—cry out to God. With great sincerity, he cried out, "O God, deliver me from being overweight and give me self-control!"

Within six months he had lost one hundred pounds,

and with God's help he has been able to stay at a healthy weight ever since.[60]

FOR FAITH

Through an honest cry to Jesus, a man whose son was possessed by an evil spirit received release for his son—and an unforgettable life lesson in faith.

When the boy was brought to Jesus, "immediately the spirit threw him into a convulsion, and falling to the ground, he began rolling around and foaming at the mouth." The father explained to Jesus that the demon often threw the boy into fire or water to destroy him.

Earlier, the father had asked the disciples of Jesus to drive out the evil spirit, but they could not. He said to Jesus, "But if You can do anything, take pity on us and help us!"

Jesus used the man's request to pinpoint his deeper need. He replied, " *'If You can?'* All things are possible to him who believes."

In the father's response to this, he seemed to be honestly probing the depths of his own heart:

> Immediately the boy's father *cried out* and said, "I do believe; help my unbelief."
>
> Jesus at once rebuked the evil spirit.
>
> After crying out and throwing him into terrible convulsions, it came out; and the boy became so

> much like a corpse that most of them said, "He is dead!" But Jesus took him by the hand and raised him; and he got up.[61]

The father's effective cry led to a major lesson in faith not only for himself, but also for the disciples of Jesus:

> He came into the house, His disciples began questioning Him privately, "Why could we not drive it out?" And He said to them, "This kind cannot come out by anything but prayer and fasting."[62]

FOR SPIRITUAL VICTORY

By crying out to God and asking Him to overcome evil's power, we seek the victory only He can provide, because He is over all the dark forces and powers which represent our true enemy. "For we do not wrestle against flesh and blood, but against principalities, against powers, against the rulers of the darkness of this age, against spiritual hosts of wickedness in the heavenly places."[63]

"When I *cry out* to You," David says, "then my enemies will turn back; this I know, because God is for me."[64]

Even the archangel Michael used his voice to invoke God's help against Satan.[65]

FOR BLESSING

Have you thought about why the prayer of Jabez was so powerful?

> And Jabez called on the God of Israel saying, "Oh, that You would bless me indeed, and enlarge my territory, that Your hand would be with me, and that You would keep me from evil, that I may not cause pain!" So God granted him what he requested.[66]

It is certainly proper to cry out to God to bless us. While wrestling with the angel of God, Jacob said, "I will not let You go unless You bless me!"

At that point, God blessed Jacob and changed his name to Israel (a name meaning "he struggles with God"). God told him, "Your name shall no longer be called Jacob, but Israel; for you have struggled with God and with men, and have prevailed."[67]

In crying out for blessing, Jacob had power with God. And it's that name *Israel* that Jabez used for his appeal: "Jabez *called on* the God of Israel."

FOR HEALING

The Lord directed the prophet Elijah to go to the town of Zarephath and lodge with a widow and her son, but later the son became seriously ill and stopped breathing. Elijah took the boy's body from his distraught mother's arms, carried him to the upstairs room where Elijah lodged, and laid him on his own bed.

The prophet knew only one thing to do.

> Then *he cried out to the LORD* and said, "O LORD my God, have You also brought tragedy on the widow with whom I lodge, by killing her son?" And he stretched himself out on the child three times, and *cried out to the LORD* and said, "O LORD my God, I pray, let this child's soul come back to him."

God responded immediately:

> Then the LORD heard the voice of Elijah; and the soul of the child came back to him, and he revived.

Not only was the boy's body healed, but the mother's faith was healed as well. In her grief and bitterness she had been ready to reject Elijah— "What have I to do with you, O man of God? Have you come to me to bring my sin to remembrance, and to kill my son?" But after Elijah brought her son down alive from the upper room, she said, "Now by this I know that you are a man of God, and that the word of the LORD in your mouth is the truth."[68]

In Jesus' day, as He came through Jericho on His way to Jerusalem, the blind beggar Bartimaeus sat by the roadside and heard the commotion of a passing crowd.

> And when he heard that it was Jesus of Nazareth, *he began to cry out* and say, "Jesus, Son of David, have mercy on me!" Then many warned him to be

> quiet; but *he cried out all the more,* "Son of David, have mercy on me!"

Jesus had Bartimaeus brought to Him. This man's need was obvious, but Jesus asked him to express it in words: "What do you want Me to do for you?"

Bartimaeus answered, "Rabboni, that I may receive my sight." The Lord rewarded his cry of faith:

> Then Jesus said to him, "Go your way; your faith has made you well." And immediately he received his sight and followed Jesus on the road.[69]

In the book of Exodus, it was after Moses cried out to the Lord for the people's physical welfare that God promised them, "I am the LORD who heals you."[70] The God of all compassion indeed hears our cry to be healed of affliction, both physical and spiritual.

FOR RELEASE FROM DEMONS

"Send her away," the disciples begged Jesus, "for she *cries out* after us."[71]

Who was this woman? She was a foreigner, a "woman of Canaan" from the region of Tyre and Sidon. But she came to Jesus "and *cried out* to Him, saying, 'Have mercy on me, O Lord, Son of David! My daughter is severely demon-possessed.'"

At first, Jesus didn't help her. He delayed His response

by saying He was sent only "to the lost sheep of the house of Israel."

This only intensified her crying. "Then she came and worshiped Him, saying, 'Lord, help me!' "

Still Jesus delayed. "It is not good to take the children's bread and throw it to the little dogs," He told her.

But she would not be quieted until her cry was answered. "Yes, Lord," she said, "yet even the little dogs eat the crumbs which fall from their masters' table."

> Then Jesus answered and said to her, "O woman, great is your faith! Let it be to you as you desire." And her daughter was healed from that very hour.[72]

Jesus' disciples might have thought of this woman as only a noisy, bothersome pest, but Jesus responded to her cry, granting her daughter's release from the grip of demons.

FOR QUENCHING OUR SPIRITUAL THIRST

After crossing the Red Sea, the people of Israel traveled three days into the wilderness without finding water. Finally they found some—but it was bitter and undrinkable. Then Moses *"cried out* to the LORD, and the LORD showed him a tree." Moses cast a branch or limb from this tree into the waters, "and the waters were made sweet."[73]

This can be spiritually true for us on many stirring occasions—in our soul-thirst we'll cry out for inner filling, and the Holy Spirit will draw our inward attention to the One "who Himself bore our sins in His own body on the tree, that we, having died to sins, might live for righteousness."[74] Then our eyes of faith will see that Christ is our all and our everything, the source and supply of our every satisfaction in time of need.

Points to Ponder

Is there any crisis in your life which you have found unsolvable? Gather several Christian friends together and cry out to God in unison for His counsel and deliverance.

Seven

For Others

Samuel cried out to the LORD for Israel,
and the LORD answered him.

1 SAMUEL 7:9

OUR CRYING OUT IS EFFECTIVE on behalf of others as well as for ourselves, as many have learned.

FOR A THEFT VICTIM

The owner of a plumbing company near Chicago kept his tools in his large truck as he drove from job to job. One day he parked his truck at a store and left the engine running as he went inside to take care of a quick business matter. When he returned a few moments later, the truck was gone.

Stunned, he called police, who chided him for leaving his truck unlocked with the engine running. They informed him that car thieves regularly circled the area looking for just such opportunities. The thieves were well organized and quickly disposed of their stolen goods. If the truck wasn't located within an hour, the plumber was told, "you might as well forget about it."

After several hours he called me for prayer. I immediately sensed that this was an opportunity for God to show His power in response to our cry. I gathered a group together and we knelt down. Our cry was simple: "Abba, Father, convict the thief and return the truck."

Two days later, the plumber received a phone call. The voice simply said, "Come and get your truck." He drove to the address in Chicago and found the truck undamaged, with checks and job orders still on the seat in the cab. Some of the tools, however, were gone.

A few days later he went to a flea market and spotted his missing tools, and he was able to recover them after proving they were his. Meanwhile, the widow of another plumber had heard about this man's plight and gave him all her husband's tools. Another friend also gave him many tools and copper fittings.

In the end, this experience gave a tremendous joy both to him and to all his friends who had cried out to God, drawing them closer to the Lord and to the reality of His promise: "Call upon Me in the day of trouble; I will deliver you, and you shall glorify Me."[75]

FOR A RUNAWAY DAUGHTER

A mother in Melbourne, Australia, was shocked and grieved when her sixteen-year-old daughter ran off with an older boy. The mother felt this boy had stolen her daughter's affections—that he had somehow convinced her to reject her family and be with him.

The mother had been trying to protect her daughter from wrong friendships and damaging decisions, and now she felt heartsick. Why had God let this happen? There seemed to be no one to whom the mother could turn for help, so she went into a room alone, put a towel over her mouth to muffle the sound of her cry, and with all her strength cried out, "O God, deliver my daughter from this boy!"

The next day the mother and father learned about one of our ministry's seminars in Melbourne, Australia. They decided to go and also to invite their daughter to attend. To their amazement, she agreed.

The daughter liked the session so much that she asked her boyfriend to go with her the next night. He came, and became so convicted that he repented of what he'd done in taking the girl away and asked both the Lord and the girl's parents to forgive him. The two young people agreed to separate from each other so that each one could grow in faith in the Lord and rebuild family relationships.

FOR A BABY STRUGGLING TO BE BORN

When the time came for the pregnant wife of one of our ministry staff members to deliver her baby, we received an urgent report that after many hours of labor, the baby was lodged in the wrong position and there was no more sign of the child's heartbeat. An emergency cesarean section was likely.

I immediately gathered several staff members and we

cried out together, asking God to deliver the baby quickly and in good health.

Shortly thereafter we received the news: The baby was delivered in good health, and without a C-section. Once again, God heard an urgent cry.

Points to Ponder

Do you ever listen to a friend tell you about a major problem and promise to pray about it—but then forget? When you remembered your lapse, did you secretly conclude that your prayer "wouldn't have counted much anyway"? If the person with the problem had been you, would you have wanted someone to cry out on your behalf? Whenever possible, cry out to the Lord with your friend immediately after he shares his need.

Eight

THE MOST IMPORTANT CRY

I will take up the cup of salvation,
and call upon the name of the LORD.

PSALM 116:13

AROUND A CERTAIN HOUSE in Jerusalem, a confused and curious crowd had suddenly gathered. They were people from lands far and wide who were visiting Jerusalem for the festival day of Pentecost. Coming forth from the house were loud praises to God, uttered in a host of languages. What was going on?

Then Peter, with the other apostles beside him, stood before the crowd and "raised his voice." He spoke to them of the Holy Spirit being poured out following the resurrection of God's chosen Messiah, Jesus of Nazareth, and bluntly declared their guilt in having crucified Jesus.[76]

He also quoted God's promise through the prophet Joel that at last was beginning to be fulfilled:

> And it shall come to pass
> That whoever *calls on the name of the LORD*
> Shall be saved.[77]

With this vital point, Peter guided the way for his listeners' appropriate response as they "were cut to the heart" by his message. Peter instructed them to repent and be baptized in the name of Jesus Christ for the remission of their sins.[78]

YOUR MOUTH AS WELL AS YOUR HEART

This crucial act of calling on the name of the Lord for salvation was something Paul later taught and explained:

> If you *confess with your mouth* the Lord Jesus and believe in your heart that God has raised Him from the dead, you will be saved. For with the heart one believes unto righteousness, and *with the mouth confession is made unto salvation....* For "*whoever calls on the name of the LORD shall be saved.*"[79]

Paul himself had cried out for salvation. In those dark days in Damascus that he would never forget, when Paul had been stricken blind by the Lord Himself, the Lord's servant Ananias came to him and in God's power restored his sight. Ananias then added, "And now why are you waiting? Arise and be baptized, and wash away your sins, *calling on the name of the LORD.*"[80]

Anyone who cries out for God's mercy in salvation will be given that mercy and salvation by the Lord. This is the promise in God's Word, "*Whoever calls on the name of the Lord shall be saved.*"

Do you remember the story Jesus told about the two men who went to the temple to pray? One man prayed within himself, reminding God of all his good works. The other cried out. He was so ashamed of his condition before a holy God that he did not even look up towards heaven. He beat his chest and said, "God, be merciful to me a sinner." Jesus told His listeners that it was the second man who went away delivered from his sin.[81]

Those who genuinely cry out to the Lord for salvation are instantly born again by the Spirit of God, who then dwells forever within them and energizes them to cry out for further needs.

And for all their remaining days they can testify, "For You, Lord, are good, and ready to forgive, and abundant in mercy to all those who *call upon You.*"[82]

Points to Ponder

When did you cry out to God for salvation in Jesus Christ? The simple act of telling that story to others has greater impact than you can begin to imagine.

Nine

THE SINCERE CRY

The LORD is near to all who call upon Him,
to all who call upon Him in truth.

PSALM 145:18

DAVID COULD SAY TO THE LORD, "Attend to my cry; give ear to my prayer which *is not from deceitful lips.*"[83] His cry was sincere.

What does such a cry represent?

A sincere cry to God, particularly during a time of great need or crisis, often represents many qualities and attitudes that God has promised to honor.

HUMILITY

To cry out with a loud voice for help—with the unleashing of emotion that often comes with it—can be a humbling experience. That's why we often resist it. We tend to be proud; we want people to think we're competent and that we've "got it all together." We don't like to admit we have a problem, much less publicly acknowledge our need for outside help to resolve it. But such pride causes God to turn away His face—"God resists the proud, but gives grace to the humble."[84]

God resists the proud because pride is our attempt to be equal with God, and it's in direct opposition to all He wants to do in and through our lives. Pride is reserving for ourselves the right to make final decisions.

Pride is building our life around ourselves…*with the cry of humility, we turn that right over to God with no strings attached.*

Pride is believing our accomplishments and successes are due to what *we* achieve…*with the cry of humility, we center our lives around God.*

Pride tries to project a polished image of competence and confidence…*with the cry of humility, we show our dependence on what God does for us and through us.*

The first quality Jesus taught His followers to cultivate was humility—to be "poor in spirit."[85] The Greek term He used depicts a roadside beggar earnestly looking to others for daily provisions. It's the quality that won the commendation of Jesus for a tax collector, as with downcast eyes this man beat his breast and cried out, "God, be merciful to me a sinner!"[86]

God "does not forget *the cry of the humble.*"[87]

One day I was speaking with a teenager who had been entrusted to us from a juvenile court. I urged him to make a commitment to obey a certain command of Scripture.

He replied, "No."

I asked him why not, and he gave a good and honest

answer: "Because I know I couldn't keep my commitment."

He was right. It's only by abiding in the Lord Jesus Christ and by God's grace and the power of His Spirit that we have the desire or ability to carry out God's will.

In that moment, I remembered God's promise that He resists the proud but gives grace to the humble. So I asked the teenager if he would be willing to find ways each day to humble himself, so that he would not resist God's grace to carry out the commitment to obey Him.

He was willing. In fact, we both got on our knees and told God that each day we would look for ways to humble ourselves before Him.

Since that day, I've begun each day by getting on my face before God and acknowledging my total unworthiness and inability to do anything for Him. I then ask Him to work in and through me.

"*Humble yourselves* therefore under the mighty hand of God," Scripture says, "that he may exalt you in due time."[88] I have learned by painful experience that if I do not humble myself, God has many others who will "volunteer" to do it for me.

ACKNOWLEDGED WEAKNESS

A sincere cry to God is an open declaration that we're incapable of dealing with a particular situation, and that we're in desperate need of His help. To cry out is to expressly acknowledge that the problem I'm facing is greater than the wisdom, ability, or strength I possess. God delights to show

His strength when we acknowledge such weakness.

An impossible crisis is often necessary to bring us to the end of our self-confidence and self-effort. As long as we struggle to solve our problems ourselves, the Lord stands by and waits, just as someone who wants to rescue a drowning person is instructed to wait until that person stops struggling, and only then is the rescuer able to pull him to shore. God allows times of crisis into our lives to remind us of our human weakness and His divine power. He wants us to cry out to Him for His supernatural work.

The more things look hopeless, the greater the possibility of God's intervention in answer to our cry, because He gets greater glory. Again and again in Scripture, the miracles of God occur in circumstances of human hopelessness.

On that evening when the wind and the waves so terrified the disciples in their boat, it's amazing that Jesus didn't rise up on His own and calm the storm at once, but instead waited until the disciples cried out for help. This is the Lord's pattern and program to keep us in close fellowship with Him and His power. He knows we don't do well with ease and prosperity. We try to become independent and live as if we don't need God.

He may allow us to keep indulging in such self-delusions and may even give us the desires of our hearts—though with "leanness" to our souls as well. But eventually we face a crisis that we recognize is clearly beyond our ability to handle. Though Satan will try to use such a situation to make us angry and bitter, God designs these "storms" to bring us back to fellowship with Him. These demanding and discouraging circumstances actually show us God's power and love as He waits for us to cry out to Him.

UNCONDITIONAL SURRENDER

The deepest, most sincere cry is one of unconditional surrender to God and His will. By crying out, we give voice and greater power to our God-given commitments and convictions, and we allow them to triumph over any idols and secret indulgences in our lives. We say, "God, You win. I surrender. I will live by Your rules, not by mine."

When we continue to cling to those idols and indulgences, God usually refuses to answer our attempted cries. We see this often in Scripture.

In the days of the prophet Jeremiah, God exposed a "conspiracy" among His people: "They have turned back to the iniquities of their forefathers who refused to hear My words, and they have gone after other gods to serve them." So God pronounced His judgment:

> Therefore thus says the LORD: "Behold, I will surely bring calamity on them which they will not be able to escape; and *though they cry out to Me, I will not listen to them.* Then the cities of Judah and the inhabitants of Jerusalem will go and *cry out to the gods to whom they offer incense,* but they will not save them at all in the time of their trouble....
>
> "So do not pray for this people, or lift up a

cry or prayer for them; for *I will not hear them in the time that they cry out to Me* because of their trouble."[89]

Our true, absolute surrender will include obedience to God's command to be His loving ambassadors in humble service to those around us, especially to those in great need. Through the prophet Isaiah, God told His people to "loose the bonds of wickedness," "undo the heavy burdens," "let the oppressed go free," "share your bread with the hungry," "bring to your house the poor who are cast out." And this promise follows:

Then you shall *call*, and the LORD will answer;
You shall *cry*, and He will say, "Here I am."[90]

COME AND HEAR

In one of the many psalms that emphasize crying out to God, an important lesson is taught to those "who fear God." The psalmist first testifies,

Come and hear, all you who fear God,
And I will declare what He has done for my soul.
I cried to Him with my mouth,
And He was extolled with my tongue.

Then the psalmist acknowledges what can block our cries from reaching God:

If I regard iniquity in my heart,
The Lord will not hear.

Finally he rests and rejoices in the knowledge that his cry has gotten through:

But certainly God has heard me;
He has attended to the voice of my prayer.
Blessed be God,
Who has not turned away my prayer,
Nor His mercy from me![91]

The iniquity represented by our pride, our self-sufficiency, and our selfishness will keep us from crying out to God in sincerity so that He will hear. But as we rest and rejoice in the forgiveness and righteousness we have through Christ, we can confidently cry out and know that God will respond.

Points to Ponder

Have you ever cried out to God in a crisis, but nothing happened? Did your cry reflect total humility? Did you acknowledge your complete weakness? Was there unconditional surrender to God's will on every matter? Are there still areas in your life where you have not fully surrendered to Him?

Ten

FERVENCY AND FAITH

"He who prays without fervency does not pray at all."

CHARLES SPURGEON

FOR MANY YEARS I WAS AWARE of my inadequate prayer life. I would read biographies of great Christians and marvel at the hours they spent in prayer. I would always feel convicted when I read the question and command Jesus gave Peter in the garden: "What, could ye not watch with me one hour? Watch and pray, that ye enter not into temptation." The next words of Jesus would give me little comfort: "The spirit indeed is willing, but the flesh is weak."[92]

Then three years ago, I followed the example of the disciples and asked, "Lord, teach me to pray."

He directed my attention to the prophet Elijah who had power with God. James tells us that Elijah "was a man subject to like passions as we are, and he prayed earnestly that it might not rain." As a result of Elijah's prayer, it didn't rain for three and a half years. Then Elijah "prayed again, and the heaven gave rain, and the earth brought forth her fruit."[93]

One word in that passage stood out to me with significance—the word *earnestly.* There was a marked intensity and fervency and seriousness to Elijah's prayer.

James introduces his account of Elijah's prayer with this statement: "The effectual fervent prayer of a righteous man availeth much."[94] The phrase "effectual fervent" is one Greek word, *energeo,* related to our English word *energy.* And the phrase "availeth much" literally means, "makes much power available." That's what this kind of fervent, earnest, energetic prayer does. Other translations render this last phrase like this: "has great power and wonderful results"; "can accomplish much"; "has great power as it is working"; "makes tremendous power available—dynamic in its working."[95]

FIRE FROM THE HEART

Much of our prayer lacks the kind of fervency God requires for effective results. But when a person sincerely cries out to God as his only hope for deliverance, provision, or protection, we can be quite certain the cry will be fervent.

Faithful preachers of God in past generations knew and taught the importance of fervor in prayer. "He who prays without fervency," Charles Spurgeon said, "does not pray at all. We cannot commune with God, who is a consuming fire, if there is no fire in our prayers." He spoke of how fervent prayer, "like a cannon planted at the gates of heaven, makes them fly open." He said it is "essential" that prayer "be red hot," and added, "Cold prayers ask the Lord not to hear them. Those who do not plead with fervency, plead not at all."[96]

"Fervency is the soul of prayer," wrote E. M. Bounds. "In prayer, fire is the motive power."[97]

"The best prayer," wrote Thomas Watson, the seventeenth-century Puritan, "is when the heart and tongue join together in concert, when they are zealous and fervent.... Fervency is to prayer as fire to incense, which makes it ascend to heaven as sweet perfume."[98]

"I cry out with my whole heart," the psalmist wrote.[99] But many of God's people in Scripture failed to do this. Through the prophet Hosea, God said, "They did not cry out to Me with their heart."[100]

When we read a parable Jesus told about a widow crying out to a judge for his help on her behalf, we're told ahead of time the parable's point: "that men always ought to pray and *not lose heart.*"[101] When we make the effort to vocalize our prayer in a cry to God, it's a good indication that we haven't lost heart.

Fervency can also be manifested in how continually we cry out to God. In a time of grief and trouble for Samuel, "he cried out to the LORD all night."[102]

TRUST AT ALL TIMES

By crying out to God, we acknowledge that He has the power and resources we require for whatever need we have or whatever trouble we're in. God delights in rewarding such faith. In fact, this quality is essential for receiving the help we lack. The more desperately we cry to God for help, the more likely we are to have faith in Him.

Fervency and faith go together. "*Trust* in Him at all times, you people," David taught. "*Pour out your heart before Him;* God is a refuge for us."[103] We show our faith and trust in Him when we pour out our hearts before Him. And God responds, "For the eyes of the LORD run to and fro throughout the whole earth, to show Himself strong on behalf of those whose heart is loyal to Him."[104]

In the words of Romans 8:15—"We cry, Abba, Father"—the Puritan Thomas Watson quickly saw the working together of fervency and faith: "'*We cry,*' there is fervency in prayer; '*Abba, Father,*' there is faith."

James tells us that we are to pray with faith, without doubting. By expressing our prayers aloud, we can often sense doubt in our own voice—an aspect that might well stay hidden if our prayers remain unspoken. Then we can confess that doubt, ask God to remove it, and cry out again in faith.

When Jesus told His disciples a parable "that men always ought to pray and not lose heart," and then spoke of God's chosen ones "who cry out day and night to Him," He quickly turned His disciples' focus to *faith:* He asked them, "when the Son of Man comes, will He really find faith on the earth?"[105]

If the Lord on that day finds His people crying out to Him, then He will indeed find faith.

Points to Ponder

Reflect on Charles Spurgeon's statement: "He who prays without fervency does not pray at all." Can you think of times when you were just "saying words" with no intensity or earnest longing? Ask the Lord to teach you to pray in the way that pleases Him.

Eleven

WHEN GOD DELAYS HIS ANSWER

I waited patiently for the LORD;
and He inclined to me, and heard my cry.

PSALM 40:1

I'VE BEEN AMAZED AT HOW just one cry will bring immediate results. But we should not always expect this to be the case. Sometimes we need to *keep* crying night and day.

A CRY FOR OUR MINISTRY

A branch of our ministry known as ALERT trains men to provide voluntary service to communities in times of natural disasters and other emergencies and needs. After several years, the program's facilities were being used to their capacity. The wife of the program's founder began to cry out to the Lord with the prayer of Jabez,[106] asking for expanded facilities.

We then learned of a large university campus for sale.

The property included more than a hundred buildings, including dormitories, administrative buildings, and a spacious gymnasium and dining area. Other features included a one-mile airstrip, a 1,000-acre farm, an 800-acre pine forest, two lakes surrounded by seventeen staff homes, a library of 130,000 volumes, a radio station, and a 220-acre RV park.

This was beyond anything we'd ever imagined—and so was the asking price! Since the beginning of our ministry in 1961, the Lord has directed us not to ask people for funds or to borrow any money. Therefore, we prayed that God would provide for this need.

A few months later, however, we experienced a "death" to our vision. Another organization signed a contract to purchase this property.

Almost three years later, we were informed that the other organization was unable to come up with the money and asked if we were still interested in buying it. We were, but we still didn't have the funds to meet the requested price. The broker responded by saying, "Make us an offer."

The vision was reborn. Two groups that had an interest in supporting us joined together to make a combined offer on the property on our behalf, much lower than the asking price. To our amazement, the offer was accepted.

It took longer than expected to work out the details of the contract, but finally it was done. Then we received an urgent message from the sellers telling us not to sign it—they had received another offer millions of dollars higher than ours.

Our hearts sank. This was "double death" to our vision.

In the midst of our distress, realizing our impossible situation, we had only one recourse—crying out to the Lord.

Several of us got on our knees and in a loud voice cried out, "O Lord, Abba, Father, deliver this property to us for Your work!" As soon as we made that cry, three words came to my mind: *Write a letter.* I wondered what possible good a letter would do to counteract an offer millions of dollars higher than ours. Yet the thought persisted, so we sat down and wrote a page-and-a-half letter of appeal, asking them to honor our offer.

We e-mailed it to the sellers. Several hours later, we received a phone call in response. The sellers had read our letter. On the basis of what we had written, they had decided to sell us the property if we could complete the transaction by the following Friday afternoon at five o'clock.

After several more times of crying out, at 4:55 that Friday afternoon, the title was transferred!

GATHERING FORCE

God's Word tells us of "His own elect who *cry out day and night* to Him," and how God will respond to them "speedily" as He patiently hears them.[107] His timely response will always come according to what *He* wisely determines is the best schedule, in reward to our faith.

Sometimes God delays His answer in order to get greater glory when the response at last comes. Sometimes He prolongs our waiting in order to intensify our fervor as we keep crying out.

Charles Spurgeon taught that "red hot" prayer means "praying perseveringly"; he said the one who prays "gathers force as he proceeds, and grows more fervent when God delays to answer."[108]

Such agonizing delays were encountered by many in Scripture—by Job, for example: "I cry out to You, but You do not answer me";[109] by David: "O My God, I cry in the daytime, but You do not hear";[110] and by Habakkuk: "O LORD, how long shall I cry, and You will not hear?"[111] All their cries, in time, were answered—and the same will be true for us.

Points to Ponder

Has God delayed His answer to some urgent cry of your heart? Ask a friend to hold you accountable to persevere in crying out—day and night, if necessary—until He answers.

Twelve

In One Accord and for His Glory

Now I plead with you, brethren,
by the name of our Lord Jesus Christ,
that you all speak the same thing.

1 Corinthians 1:10

FIVE TIMES IN THE OPENING CHAPTERS OF ACTS we're told that the disciples were in "one accord." This was also true in their crying out to the Lord: "They raised their voice to God with one accord."[112]

In the Old Testament, in a time of great need for God's people, the Lord gave these instructions through the prophet Joel:

> Consecrate a fast,
> Call a sacred assembly;
> Gather the elders
> And all the inhabitants of the land

Into the house of the LORD your God,
And *cry out to the LORD.*[113]

They were to gather in God's house and give voice to their united prayer. Then Joel himself set the example for them: "O LORD, to You I *cry out.*"[114]

When an entire group cries out in right relationship with the Lord and with each other, they're in one accord, and powerful results take place. The difference between the prayer we commonly experience in a prayer meeting and the true one-accord crying out that took place in the first-century church is like the difference between diffused light and a laser beam! When one person leads a group in prayer, those who listen are often distracted by other thoughts and concerns. But when the entire group focuses on an urgent need and cries out in unison, there's little chance of distraction.

CRYING OUT IN UNISON

A church in Oklahoma City began including a time of united crying out to God in their regular weekly services. Soon afterward, a man in the church asked that the congregation call out to the Lord regarding his physical condition. He had contracted a viral disease that damaged his ability to walk. For a year, he was dependent on a wheelchair or walker to get around. Seventeen different doctors had been unable to help him.

The entire congregation cried out in unison, "O Lord, deliver this man from his infirmity." At the end of the prayer time, he felt his whole body strengthened. He walked forward and gave a public testimony of God's healing power, and walked out of the church holding his walker over his head. This caused the entire church and all who knew him to glorify God.

"WITH ONE MOUTH"

When Jesus taught His disciples to pray, He told them to say "Our Father," not "My Father." In our praying we should always keep in mind that we're in a covenant with all the members of the body of Christ, so that when one member is blessed, all the members benefit. The awareness of our bond together is particularly true when believers cry out in unison, as well as when we praise God together, according to God's design: "that you may with one mind and *one mouth* glorify the God and Father of our Lord Jesus Christ."[115]

Whether alone or in company with God's children, we cry out to Him in our need, and then experience His help and deliverance.

And what then? We give Him all the glory through our gratitude and praise.

TESTIFYING TO HIS WONDERFUL WORKS

This goal of drawing attention to God's glory through our trials, our cries, and His answers is fully encompassed in God's invitation in His Word: "Call upon Me in the day of trouble; I will deliver you, and *you shall glorify Me.*"[116] Significantly, the verse preceding this invitation tells us,

"Offer to God thanksgiving, and pay your vows to the Most High."[117]

God's ultimate purpose in all creation is to demonstrate His glory. We help fulfill that purpose by telling others of His love and power at work in our lives: "Let the redeemed of the LORD say so, whom He has redeemed from the hand of the enemy."[118]

The voice that has been bold to cry out to the Lord God in prayer will more likely be bold to speak aloud both to testify of the Lord's work in our lives, and also to share the Lord's gospel (His greatest work!) with the people around us.

As we cry out to God and we receive His answers, let's look for ways to share the results with others. (A special Web site has been prepared that will report the mighty power of God in the lives of those who cry out to Him. To submit your report, log on to www.lifestudygroups.com/contact.asp.)

OUR VOICES LIFTED IN PRAISE

In Scripture, crying out is practiced not only in seeking God's help but also in fervently praising Him, to His glory. We see it often in the Old Testament, and we see it again when Jesus entered Jerusalem on Palm Sunday:

> Then the multitudes who went before and those who followed *cried out,* saying: "Hosanna to the Son of David! 'Blessed is He who comes in the name of the LORD!' Hosanna in the highest!"[119]

The Lord is determined to hear voices crying out in His praise to Him—so much so that when the Pharisees that day complained about the noise Jesus was arousing among the people, He answered, "I tell you that if these should keep silent, the stones would immediately *cry out.*"[120]

THE CRIES IN OUR FUTURE

In heaven, where all our hearts will be pure and God-centered, we'll continue to cry out—not for deliverance, but in praise. Heaven won't be a quiet place! In the portrait we find in Revelation, John reveals what he heard from the voices of the redeemed in eternity:

> I looked, and behold, a great multitude which no one could number, of all nations, tribes, peoples, and tongues, standing before the throne and before the Lamb, clothed with white robes, with palm branches in their hands, and *crying out with a loud voice,* saying, "Salvation belongs to our God who sits on the throne, and to the Lamb!"...
>
> And there were *loud voices* in heaven, saying, "The kingdoms of this world have become the kingdoms of our Lord and of His Christ, and He shall reign forever and ever!"...
>
> After these things I heard *a loud voice of a great multitude* in heaven, saying, "Alleluia! Salvation and glory and honor and power belong to the Lord our God!"...

> And I heard, as it were, the voice of a great multitude, as the sound of many waters and as the sound of mighty thunderings, saying, "Alleluia! For the Lord God Omnipotent reigns!"[121]

We can begin this fervent praise even now by making sure we give Him glory with our voices.

The psalmist shouts to us,

> Oh, bless our God, you peoples!
> And make the voice of His praise *to be heard.*[122]

And in the final verse of the very last Psalm, the verse that brings to conclusion that entire songbook of heartfelt cries, God's Word says this: "Let everything that has breath praise the LORD."[123]

You and I have the gift of breath from God…and we can forever offer it back to Him in spoken praise.

Praise His mighty name!

Points to Ponder

> Suggest to your Bible study, Sunday school class, or small group that they consider the principles in this book and begin crying out in unison for urgent needs as they arise within the group.

One Final Thought

Seek the LORD *while He may be found,*
call upon Him while He is near.

ISAIAH 55:6

PERHAPS THIS WHOLE IDEA of "crying out" still feels a little strange, a little uncomfortable to you.

Perhaps you've bought into the prevailing notion that a person's faith is very personal and private. So you've kept your beliefs to yourself. You've kept your faith to yourself. You've kept your prayers to yourself. You've kept and restrained your praise and gratitude to God as something extremely private and completely silent.

Through it all, you've been dignified, calm, proper, respectable, and restrained.

But maybe you've also begun to feel a little empty sometimes...as if God was very distant and far away from you...and you've even begun to wonder if He's hearing your prayers at all.

A friend of mine recently described his own experience with giving loud voice to his prayers. With his wife suffering from cancer and other family problems looming, he took a long walk down a dirt road in a nearby forest.

Faraway from prying eyes and listening ears, he determined to lift his voice to God and cry aloud his fears and hopes and requests before the Lord. At first, he later admitted, he felt strange, a little foolish—even self-conscious—about it. His doubts kept telling him that it was "just a gimmick," and that it really wouldn't make any difference.

But he began to do it anyway.

Kneeling on the forest floor, he began to cry aloud to the Lord.

Immediately, something happened. Tears sprang to his eyes. The sense of urgency and fear he'd been feeling for weeks on end began spilling—and then gushing—out before God. He felt more like a child with his father than he could remember for a long time. "I can't explain it," he told me, "but praying that way made a difference in *me.* It changed the whole nature of my prayers."

Crying out is now an important part of my friend's prayer life. But it would have never happened if—all by himself out in that pine forest—he hadn't swallowed his pride, set aside his doubts, and humbled himself before the Lord.

Maybe that's where it could start for you, too. Take your anxieties and burdens and worries before your heavenly Father. Humble yourself and cry aloud to Him with all your heart.

He will hear you, just as He has promised. And your life will begin to change from that hour.

The publisher and author would love to hear your comments about this book. *Please contact us at:* www.lifechangebooks.com

NOTES

1. Luke 18:1–8
2. *Dallas Morning News,* October 28, 2001; reprinted with permission.
3. Psalm 50:15
4. Psalm 145:18
5. Psalm 55:17
6. Psalm 18:6
7. Psalm 34:15
8. Psalm 34:17
9. Psalm 61:1
10. Psalms 3:4; 30:2
11. Psalms 4:3; 28:1–2
12. Psalm 142:1
13. Galatians 4:6; see also Romans 8:15
14. Isaiah 31:4
15. Isaiah 38:14; 59:11
16. Isaiah 16:7; Jeremiah 48:31
17. Psalms 35:28; 37:30; Proverbs 8:7
18. Joshua 1:8
19. Psalm 1:2
20. Romans 8:15
21. Romans 8:34
22. Romans 8:26–27
23. Psalm 38:9
24. Luke 8:43–48
25. 1 Samuel 1:10, 12–13, 15
26. Charles Spurgeon, in a sermon delivered September 8, 1881, at London's Metropolitan Tabernacle.
27. See the disciple Ananias's prayer in Acts 9:14.
28. Romans 10:12; 1 Corinthians 1:2
29. Exodus 2:23–25
30. Exodus 3:7–8
31. Exodus 14:10
32. Judges 3:8–9; 3:14–15; 4:3
33. Judges 10:9–16
34. Judges 10:16
35. Judges 11:1
36. Psalm 22:4–5
37. Daniel 9:3
38. Daniel 9:17–19
39. Psalm 107:6; see also verses 13, 19, and 28
40. Psalm 50:15
41. 2 Corinthians 12:10
42. Psalm 46:1
43. Psalm 102:1–2
44. Matthew 8:23–27; Luke 8:22–25
45. Matthew 14:30–31
46. Jonah 2:2

47. 1 Chronicles 5:20
48. Psalm 88
49. Psalm 88:18, ESV, TLB, and NASB
50. Psalm 88:1–2,9,13
51. Exodus 22:22–23
52. Psalm 72:12
53. Proverbs 21:13
54. Exodus 22:22–24
55. Deuteronomy 24:14–15
56. Psalm 20:1
57. Psalm 138:3
58. See Luke 6:27; Matthew 5:48; 2 Corinthians 13:11, KJV; Ephesians 4:1–2; 1 Peter 1:16; 1 Thessalonians 5:17; Luke 10:27
59. Proverbs 2:3
60. You can check out the account on Ken's Web site: http://kenpierpont.com
61. Mark 9:17–27, NASB
62. Mark 9:28–29, KJV
63. Ephesians 6:12
64. Psalm 56:9
65. Jude 9
66. 1 Chronicles 4:10
67. Genesis 32:26–29
68. 1 Kings 17:17–24
69. Mark 10:46–52
70. Exodus 15:26
71. Matthew 15:23
72. Matthew 15:21–28
73. Exodus 15:25
74. 1 Peter 2:24
75. Psalm 50:15
76. Acts 2
77. Acts 2:21
78. Acts 2:37–38
79. Romans 10:9–10, 13
80. Acts 22:16
81. Luke 18:9–14
82. Psalm 86:5
83. Psalm 17:1
84. James 4:6
85. Matthew 5:3
86. Luke 18:13
87. Psalm 9:12
88. 1 Peter 5:6, KJV
89. Jeremiah 11:9–14
90. Isaiah 58:6–9
91. Psalm 66:16–20
92. Matthew 26:40–41, KJV
93. James 5:17–18, KJV
94. James 5:16, KJV
95. James 5:16, TLB, NASB, ESV, AMP
96. Charles Spurgeon, *Morning and Evening*

97. E. M. Bounds, *The Necessity of Prayer*
98. Thomas Watson, *The Lord's Prayer*
99. Psalm 119:145
100. Hosea 7:14
101. Luke 18:1
102. 1 Samuel 15:11
103. Psalm 62:8
104. 2 Chronicles 16:9
105. Luke 18:1–8
106. Be sure to read Dr. Bruce Wilkinson's life-changing book, *The Prayer of Jabez.*
107. Luke 18:7–8
108. Charles Spurgeon, *Morning and Evening*
109. Job 30:20
110. Psalm 22:2
111. Habakkuk 1:2
112. Acts 4:24
113. Joel 1:14
114. Joel 1:19
115. Romans 15:6
116. Psalm 50:15
117. Psalm 50:14
118. Psalm 107:2
119. Matthew 21:9
120. Luke 19:40
121. Revelation 7:9–10; 11:15; 19:1, 6
122. Psalm 66:8
123. Psalm 150:6

EXPERIENCE THE POWER OF CRYING OUT
IN YOUR OWN LIFE STUDY GROUP

STEPS YOU CAN TAKE

1. Form a group in your church, home, business, or community.
2. Meet once a week to study forty-nine commands of Christ.
3. Watch a powerful video message on each command by outstanding Bible teachers.
4. Discuss the character quality that relates directly to the command of Christ.
5. Set goals on applying the command and character quality.
6. Conclude with prayer and crying out for special needs.

THE RICH REWARDS OF THIS STUDY

- The Commands of Christ are *The Curriculum of the Great Commission*—"Teach them all things I have commanded you."
- You will know Christ more intimately—"He that hath my commandments, and keepeth them, he it is that loveth me: and he that loveth me shall be loved of my Father, and I will love him, and will manifest myself to him" (John 14:21).
- Experience true joy—"These things [*commands*] have I spoken unto you…that your joy might be full" (John 15:11).

For More Information…

on Life Study Groups, to order resources online, and to post needs for and results from crying out, visit:

www.lifestudygroups.com